Wildlife Wong
and the
Fig Wasp

by
Dr Sarah Pye

Wildlife Wong and the Fig Wasp
August 2022

ISBN: 978-0-6451543-6-8 (paperback)
ISBN: 978-0-6451543-7-5 (ebook)

Published by:

Estralita Publishing
ABN: 86 230 144 690
86/7 Grand Parade, Parrearra, QLD, 4575
⊕ www.sarahrpye.com

Copyright:
Text: © Sarah Pye
Sketches: © Ali Beck
Photographs: © copyright details accompany each image. Author holds copyright for all un-attributed images.

All rights reserved. No part of this book may be reproduced in any form or by any means, except for brief citation or review, without prior written permission from the author via www.sarahrpye.com.

Pencil sketch illustrator: *Ali Beck*
Cover design: *Gram Telen*
Layout design: *Gram Telen*
Wildlife Wong cartoon illustrator: *Isuru Pltawala*
Cover fig wasp photo: *Chun Xing Wong*
Cover author photo: *Amber Grant*

 A catalogue record for this work is available from the National Library of Australia

Check out what other kids think about this book...

"I loved this story so much and learned so many amazing things! For example, how long (/short!) fig wasps live and what their jobs are. I learned that if you see a little tree, it may have grown from another tree's roots, so it may be much, much older than you think!

It was very funny when Wildlife Wong thought he had dropped a grain of rice on a stick, but the stick went for a walk and then camouflaged itself again!

I would definitely recommend this fantastic book to everyone, including kids who are home schooling like me, and adults like my mum who loved it too, especially as she's from Borneo.

I can't wait to do the science experiments at the end of the book!"

Reuben, age 9

"I really love this book. It has lots of different things I like. I got to learn about new things and facts that aren't talked about in school. There are also lots of things that make you laugh and mystery and suspense.

It is also great how the book also mentions animals from the other books such as the sun bear. It is easy to read and teaches you new and tricky words that make you feel smarter and make you want to keep reading. I love that I have all of Wildlife Wong's books, so far!"

Elke, age 9

"I loved reading the book. It was great and it has a lot of detail in it and has a lot you can learn about the fig wasp. It is fun to read, and I think it is the best book about fig wasps, sun bears and other forest creatures. I think it is a book for everyone to read and enjoy."

James, age 10

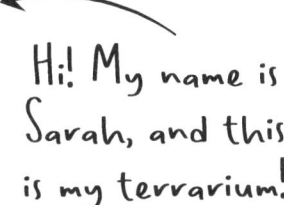

Hi! My name is Sarah, and this is my terrarium!

This is the fifth book about Wildlife Wong. Don't worry if you haven't read the other books because you don't have to read them in order.

This book includes a story about my friend Wildlife Wong, lots of cool facts, and interesting activities so you can pretend you are a scientist just like Wong. You can make your own terrarium on page 61!

There are videos of the experiments on my website www.sarahrpye.com. You can also download pages for your own **Nature Journal** and a template for making a **unique** cover. Does that sound like fun? I'll remind you again at the end!

Introducing Wildlife Wong

Wildlife Wong is a tropical forest **ecologist**. That's the name for a scientist who studies how plants, animals and humans live together. If you see a bold word (like ecologist), you can check out its meaning at the back of the book. He lives on an island called Borneo. Perhaps you can search on the internet and find out how far away Borneo is from where you live!

Can you see Borneo on this map?

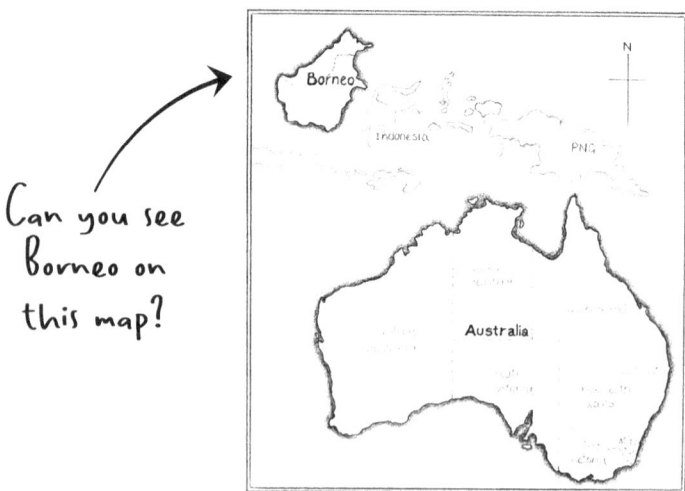

What's important about Borneo?

Borneo is a magical island. It is home to over 15,000 different species of plants, or **flora**, and over 1,000 species of animals, or **fauna**. Many of them only live on Borneo. This island is home to the smallest **mammal** on Earth (humans are a type of mammal); the largest flower on Earth; and the largest **invertebrate** on Earth (an invertebrate is an animal without a skeleton). One of them is the super-amazing fig wasp, the star of this story!

There are many other amazing flora and fauna in Borneo that you probably didn't know existed. Every single one of them is important to life in the rainforest. Humans can learn all kinds of things from other species and one of the most important is how to work together.

That doesn't mean animals are always best friends because they have three things on their minds: They need to find enough food to eat, they need to make sure they don't get eaten, and they also want to make sure they keep their species alive by having babies. These three things are called **predation, preservation,** and **procreation**.

Wildlife Wong And The Fig Wasp

The three Ps!

See if you can find examples of these happening as you read the story.

Living in the rainforest

At the time of our story, Wong lived in a small house with a white wooden railing at a place called Danum Valley Conservation Centre. His little house was surrounded by more houses where other scientists lived. Some of them were studying trees. Others were studying lizards, and some were studying birds. Wildlife Wong was the only person studying sun bears. Beyond the houses was a thick, dark rainforest.

Do you like Wong's house in the rainforest?

PHOTOGRAPH: © WONG SIEW TE

Learning from animals

Wildlife Wong wanted to find out things about sun bears that no-one knew. To do that, he needed to trap them, put a collar around their necks, set them free and follow them. Unfortunately, sun bears are very good at hiding and Wong was worried because, so far, he had only caught three bears! This sounds like the *Goldilocks* story, doesn't it?

It was much easier to trap wild pigs (called bearded pigs), so Wong decided to study them too.

Aren't sun bears cute?

There was something else worrying Wong. All three bears he caught in his trap had been **malnourished**, which means they were really thin and unwell. And all three bears had died, which made Wong feel very sad. The bearded pigs he managed to catch were also so thin he could see their rib bones through their skin. Wong didn't know why they were all so sick. It was a puzzle, and he was racing against time to find the answer. Nature was like a detective story sometimes, and Wildlife Wong was the detective. He didn't know it then, but the answer had something to do with a very tiny flying creature called a fig wasp.

Private investigator

One day Wong and his assistant Chia-Chien (who is now his wife) trapped a fourth bear in his barrel trap. They gave it medicine to make it sleep, then took it out of the trap and measured things like its length, **girth** (distance around his waist), weight, and temperature. They worked quickly so the bear didn't wake up. As soon as the male bear started moving, they put him softly on the ground and moved away to watch from a distance. Wong named his new bear *Lai Xiung*, which sounds like *lye-shoong* and means *Come Bear* in Chinese. He hoped the name would make this bear easier to find!

Wong and Chia-Chien trapping bears.

PHOTOGRAPH: © WONG SIEW TE

A few days later, on a very humid day, Wong woke up in his comfy bed. He really wanted to turn over and go back to sleep, but this was the day he was going on a bear hunt to find answers. Wong felt rain coming, and he knew it would be more difficult to track the sun bear if the rain washed away tracks and bear poo. So, he dragged himself out of bed, ate, cleaned his breakfast dishes quickly and prepared for a day in the forest.

First, he put a large battery into the bottom of his backpack with a long wire attached. Then he put a plastic lunch box containing last night's leftover fried rice on top and scrunched his rain jacket around it to keep it cool. Next came his binoculars. He shoved a drink bottle of water and a couple of empty Ziplock bags into one side pocket, and his notebook, pen and compass in the other. Last, he slid his folded **topographic** map into the outside pocket. (A topographic map shows natural things like hills and stream, not roads and buildings.)

Wong put his arms through the shoulder straps then picked up a large **antenna** in the shape of the letter H. It was connected to the wire from the battery. With his other hand, he picked up the VHF radio receiver. (VHF stands for Very High Frequency.) The receiver would pick up a signal sent by the bear's collar so he could follow it.

Wildlife Wong And The Fig Wasp

Before he entered the forest, Wong raised his antenna as high as his arm would allow and turned on the radio receiver. Perhaps he would be lucky, and his bear would be right around the corner. He slowly turned in a circle. If the steady beeping noise grew louder, he knew he was pointing the antenna towards Lai Xiung. A few days before, another scientist had seen a sun bear wandering around the rubbish dump, but Wong wasn't as lucky this time. He collapsed the antenna, strapped it to the outside of his pack, and headed into the forest. The earth was damp, and his hiking boots squeaked as he walked.

Wong using an H-antenna to track animals.

PHOTOGRAPH: © WONG SIEW TE

Wildlife Wong And The Fig Wasp

At first, Wong found the path through the forest easily, but the deeper he got into the forest, the more overgrown it became, and the slower he moved. He pushed branches aside and waved his arm back and forth in front of his face to break cobwebs made by busy spiders during the night. He brushed past wet leaves, spraying himself with perfect, round droplets of dew that hung from them like jewels. He clambered down a muddy gully and followed the trail left by the last flash flood six months before. All sorts of **debris** (which sounds like *d-bree* and means scattered rubbish) had been washed downstream. He could tell how high the water had come from twigs, branches, and grasses left high in the trees. If he had been here then, he would have been underwater! The riverbed smelt musty, like dirty socks.

Mid-morning, Wong stopped on the muddy bank and glanced down at his dirty boots. A striped tiger leech about as long as your little finger had climbed up the ladder of his laces. It balanced on the end of its body, sniffing the air, and was just about to latch onto his ankle. Wong reached down and picked off its squashy body. He rolled it around into a ball between his thumb and forefinger, just like you would with chewing gum which has lost its flavour, and flicked it into the rainforest. The leech would have to find life-giving blood somewhere else!

Leeches need to drink blood to live!

PHOTOGRAPH: © WONG SIEW TE

Wong unpacked his H-antenna and swept in a circle again. Nothing. He would have more luck if he was at the top of the fire tower. From there, he would have a view of the entire valley. So, he repacked his bag and pulled his way out of

Wildlife Wong And The Fig Wasp

the riverbed, grabbing **saplings**, or small trees, for support.

Halfway up the slope, Wong caught a whiff of something dead. His heart started beating fast in his chest. He hoped it wasn't Lai Xiung, but he needed to find out, so he followed his nose. The smell became stronger and stronger. It was very unpleasant, and Wong pulled his shirt over his nostrils. Then he saw something very strange. It looked like the end of a sword covered in dust, coming out of an open scallop shell, and it smelt really bad. As he drew closer, he realised it was actually a flower. Each of the two petals was the size of a small plate with white in the middle and pinky-purple around the edge. The part that looked like the end of a sword was so tall it reached his hips. Even though he was trying not to breathe the **putrid** (or horrible) air, Wildlife Wong was excited to see it because this was a very rare plant known as the **corpse** flower. (Corpse is the name for a dead body… can you guess how it got that name?)

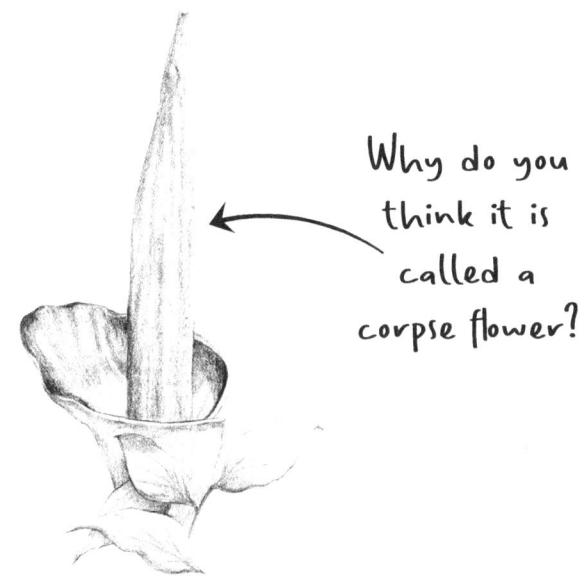

Why do you think it is called a corpse flower?

Wong peered closer. There were heaps of insects buzzing around the smelly flower. Some of them **gorged** themselves with food (or ate until they were full), then flew away with pollen stuck to their bodies. When they were hungry again, he suspected they might land on another corpse flower and leave pollen behind, helping the flower grow seeds. It seemed the flower and the flies couldn't live without each other.

Wong was relieved. The smell hadn't been a dead sun bear, or even a dead bearded pig.

Wildlife Wong And The Fig Wasp

It was time to continue on his bear hunt, but he wasn't sure which direction to head next, so he swung his antenna in a circle. This time the beeping was stronger, which **indicated** (or told him) which direction to walk.

As Wildlife Wong left the stinky flower behind, he could hear small birds called barbets calling in the distance. "*Took, took, tarook*", they said. Wildlife Wong knew barbets usually got really excited when they found a fruiting fig tree. The sound came from the same direction as his bear, and he had a good feeling about that, so he walked a little faster. Maybe he was close to finding some answers!

Tracking animals is all about **observation** (or looking really carefully) so Wong scanned the ground as he moved. A little further, he found a tree stump. It was surrounded by chips of orange wood and sawdust. His bear had been here, using his claws to break the wood apart and licking up tasty termites with his tongue. It wasn't long ago, because the woodchips were still bright colours, but a pill millipede was already crawling through them. The newly created, dark, moist caverns would make a perfect place to lay her eggs. She felt the ground shake as Wong grew closer which scared her. Within a millisecond, the millipede had rolled into a ball and locked her armour into place for safety. She didn't move until he was gone.

Wong was amazed by the pill millipede's armour.

Photograph: © Wong Siew Te

A tree is an entire community

Wong pushed a branch aside and before him was a gigantic fig tree. It looked like the mother of the forest. All kinds of leaves, lichen and fungi were growing on its trunk, and insects buzzed past his ears. These were fig wasps, but they didn't look like wasps you might be used to. They were much smaller, and their bodies were glossy black.

As he moved closer to the tree, the VHF beeping grew louder. Wildlife Wong put down his pack, took out his binoculars and squinted up into the **foliage** (which sounds like *foh-lee-edge* and means leaves). He could see fat, round, purple fruits growing straight from its trunk. He spied his bear about 50m above the ground having a rest. Lai Xiung's full belly was flat against a thick branch and his legs were hanging down.

The bear was not alone. A feast was underway. To the left of the bear, some of the noisy barbets were snacking. A colourful Atlas moth flew by. The tip of its unusual wings looked like snake heads! On the end of a branch, Wong **glimpsed** the real thing — a venomous pit viper snake trying to sneak up on the barbets while they were eating. It was hungry too, but not for figs!

Wildlife Wong And The Fig Wasp

A sneaky snake!

PHOTOGRAPH: © WONG SIEW TE

Lai Xiung had fallen asleep. Wong thought it was probably because he had eaten too many figs, but he hadn't seen a bear eat figs before and science is all about proof. So, he walked quietly around the base of the tree, shooing away wasps, and looking for bear **scats**, or poo. Luckily, it hadn't rained yet, and he could learn a lot from poo. If Lai Xiung had eaten the figs, his **excrement** (another word for poo) would look like a cow pat dotted with seeds. If, instead, he had been eating termites or earthworms, the **faeces** (yeah, another word for poo!) would be the colour of dirt: more solid and dotted with tiny termite skeletons.

Wildlife Wong And The Fig Wasp

On the far side of the tree, Wong found a soft poo sample with seeds. It seemed his bear *had* been eating figs. He took a plastic bag from his backpack and scooped it up so he could peer at it through his microscope when he got back to the **laboratory** (a place where scientists work). He zipped the plastic bag tight so it wouldn't leak and shoved it in his cargo pants' pocket.

Lai Xiung was still sleeping, so Wong walked towards the **buttress root** of another nearby fig tree, where he had full view of the sleeping bear. He squashed his ear against the root and almost thought he could hear the two trees talking to each other underground through their fungi-covered roots. He turned his head and looked straight up the tall trunk. The figs on this second tree were smaller and unripe. A buzz of activity was taking place above him. Before his eyes, a fig wasp landed on one of the figs and disappeared inside through a tiny tunnel the tree had left for this very purpose.

Wildlife Wong And The Fig Wasp

Figs grow straight from the trunk.

Wildlife Wong reached high on the trunk, pulled off one of the hard balls, and broke it open with his thumbnails. The inside looked like hundreds of tiny flowers. He thought back to the corpse flower and how the flies helped it transport pollen to other flowers. How was pollen spread from the male to the female fig flowers if they were all locked away inside this hard ball? Was that what the tiny wasp was doing when she tunnelled inside?

Wong squinted. Right in the middle of the miniature flowers, he could see about 10 tiny fig wasp **larvae**. Did that mean they were born inside this cocoon? How did they get out? What if they didn't get out to pollinate another fig? Did that mean there would be no figs? And if there were no figs, what would his sun bear eat? Wildlife Wong had more questions than he started with. He was starting to suspect fig wasps were very important.

PHOTOGRAPH: © CHUN XING WONG

The art of deception

Trying to solve problems makes me hungry, and watching others eat also sometimes makes me hungry. Do they make you hungry?

Wildlife Wong's stomach growled so, while he waited for Lai Xiung to wake up, he sat down, leaning against the giant root. He took last night's leftovers out of his backpack and had his own feast. Food always seemed tastier the second day. A few small grains of rice fell from his chopsticks onto a nearby twig. At least, he thought it was a twig until the twig moved!

Things in the rainforest are not always what they seem. Some animals, like this stick insect, make themselves look like something completely different, so predators can't find them. This is called **camouflage**. Wong knew one reptile, called the chameleon lizard (*cam-eel-ee-en*), even changes its colour to match the leaves it is sitting on, and disappears just like it is wearing an invisibility cloak!

Wong used camouflage too. He smiled as he looked down at his army cargo pants, which helped him blend into the rainforest. He realised humans have stolen a few tricks from insects! This is called **biomimicry** (which sounds like *bio-mimik-ree*).

Wong has a species of stick insect named after him. Isnt that cool?

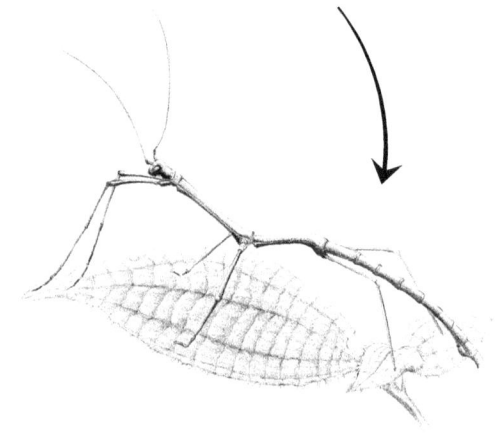

Wildlife Wong watched the stick insect **scuttle**, or run fast, into a bush. Then, before his eyes, it froze like a statue so he could no longer see where it was. "That's fantastic camouflage!" he said out loud to no one.

Wildlife Wong And The Fig Wasp

The strongest animal in the forest

Wong looked down at his feet where the grains of rice had landed. A tiny army of ants walked across the path in single file. They reached the grain of rice, which was as big as they were. Instead of diverting around the outside, one ant lifted the heavy load on top of its back. Wong wished he could lift something bigger than he was. The ant continued walking in the line, followed closely behind by his friends, who propped him up when he stumbled. Before long, all the spilt rice from Wong's lunch was moving. He followed the **procession** with his eyes until each grain disappeared down a hole to an ant city below the surface. Wong wished he could shrink himself so he could follow them down the hole and see what happened to his lunch next. Maybe the ants were planning a party?

Wildlife Wong And The Fig Wasp

One big jigsaw

Wildlife Wong marvelled at the scene before him, and at how it all fit together like a jigsaw puzzle.

All the animals and plants seemed to work together. Just like the corpse flower needed flies, the fig tree seemed to need the tiny superhero fig wasp. Without the tiny wasps buzzing around his head, he wondered if there would be no figs for sun bears and birds to eat.

Have you ever got really close to finishing a jigsaw puzzle, and there is one piece missing? It's annoying, isn't it? Well, nature is just like a jigsaw puzzle. It needs every single piece to work properly. This is called **biodiversity**. Wildlife Wong wondered if there was a jigsaw piece missing, and it was causing the bears and pigs to starve. He hoped he could find out before the bears and pigs were gone.

After forty minutes resting Lai Xiung climbed down to a smaller branch. He used his right paw to reach for figs and stuffed them into his mouth whole. It was the first time Wong had actually **witnessed** (or seen) a bear eating figs. This was proof that bears ate figs. He was so excited that he didn't notice a flash of orange as a mother orangutan arrived at the tree with her infant clinging tightly to the hair on her chest. She wanted to eat in peace and was not happy having human company, so she started breaking off twigs and throwing them at him like spears. Ouch! Wong wrapped his arms over his head and stayed where he was for about five minutes. He hoped she would get used to him being there. But the sticks hurt, and he was finally chased away.

Orangutan means man of the forest!

As Wildlife Wong made his way back towards the research centre, the shadows got longer and longer, and the forest grew darker and darker. The track looked completely different, and he used his compass to make sure he was going the right way. As he walked, he wondered if the wasps slept at night. He passed a tree

Wildlife Wong And The Fig Wasp

with tiny fungi growing up its trunk. They were glowing in the dark and attracting a different community of tiny insects! Wong turned his headlamp on and listened for breaking twigs. He didn't belong in the rainforest at night, and he certainly did not want to end up prey for a **nocturnal** clouded leopard.

The path widened. It meant he was nearly home. Noisy insects called cicadas sent a wave of ear-splitting sound across the valley. Then flying frogs, high in the trees, started booming. They were always loud when rain was coming. Before his eyes, the rainforest was transforming into another wonderland.

Wildlife Wong stepped out into the clearing. He could see welcoming lights from the research centre, and he walked towards them. His day in the forest had answered some of his questions, but it had created others. He had more detective work to do, especially about fig wasps, but first he had to sleep.

Wildlife Wong And The Fig Wasp

What did Wildlife Wong learn from fig wasps?

The next day, Wong went to the library. He pulled down a thick book about trees and turned to the page of figs. What he read was amazing! Could it really be true that some fig wasps were born and died in the same fig, and never ever saw the light of day?

At lunchtime, Wong chatted to a scientist called Norhiyati Ahmad (or Yati for short). Yati was trying to find out if the weather effected tree fruiting. She was conducting a **longitudinal** study. Longitudinal means she was comparing the changes over time. Yati told him that the tropical rainforest trees in Borneo usually took turns growing fruit all year round. This was especially true for fig trees because they needed to **coordinate** (or work with) fig wasps. Fig wasps only live a couple of days, and they were on a race against time. The female wasps had to hatch inside a fig, grow up, find their way out of the fig, find another fig, tunnel inside and lay their eggs before they died. The tree helped by making sure there were figs ready at all times!

Yati discovered that sometimes rainforest trees talked to each other and decided to fruit at the same time. Over a few weeks, eighty percent of the trees flowered in **unison,** which means together. This was called **mass fruiting.** Although there were still plenty of figs for fig wasps all year, the big rainforest animals (like sun bears, orangutans and bearded pigs) loved the mass fruiting! They stuffed themselves like you do at a birthday party. Yati also found that the trees grew more flowers (and then fruit) in years where there was very little rain.

Aren't baby bearded pigs adorable?

Wildlife Wong And The Fig Wasp

Wong started helping Yati gather more data and together they found there had been no mass fruiting for the last four years. There was still some food for the animals, because the fig wasps and fig trees still did their thing, but it seemed there was not enough. It was like a supermarket with half the shelves empty. That's why he had seen so many animals in one fig tree, and that's why the animals he trapped were starving. Wong discovered something else too: The mass flowering sent a message to bearded pigs.

When flower petals fell down and covered the rainforest floor like carpet, the bearded pigs mated. In the same time it took for the flowers to turn to fruit, baby piglets grew big inside their mums. So, when the mother pigs gave birth, there was plenty of food for their piglets. Maybe, thought Wong, if there was too much food *all* the time, there would also be too many pigs. He wondered if the times of **famine** (when there wasn't enough food) helped keep the natural balance. It seemed he and Yati had found another piece of the puzzle.

The more Wong learnt, the more amazing the rainforest became. He never looked at the beautiful tall fig trees the same way again. Now he treats them like the mothers of the forest who keep the peace and make sure everyone gets fed. But he also realises the mighty trees can't do this important work alone. Without tiny fig wasps, the sun bears, orangutans, and bearded pigs might become extinct. It turns out fig wasps are the hidden heroes in the rainforest.

Important animals in small packages!

PHOTOGRAPH: © CHUN XING WONG

Who's who in the rainforest?

Did you enjoy that story? Now, why don't we learn a bit more about some of the creatures in the rainforest. THEN, it's your turn to become a scientist and conduct experiments!

The rainforest in Borneo is home to the world's smallest bear and the world's smallest elephant. It is home to the world's largest flower and the world's largest stick insect. It is also home to the hero of our story, the tiny, mighty fig wasp. Let me introduce you to some characters you met in the story.

What's special about trees?

It goes without saying, but there wouldn't be a rainforest without trees. Trees have been around for about 300 million years, (that's 3,000 times longer than humans), and there are about

60,000 different trees on Earth. About 3,000 of them are in the Bornean rainforest.

Because they are really different from us, and don't seem to do a lot, some people don't take much notice of trees. That's a pity because trees are really cool. They don't have eyes, ears, a mouth or a brain, but they still watch, listen, communicate and eat. How do you think they do that?

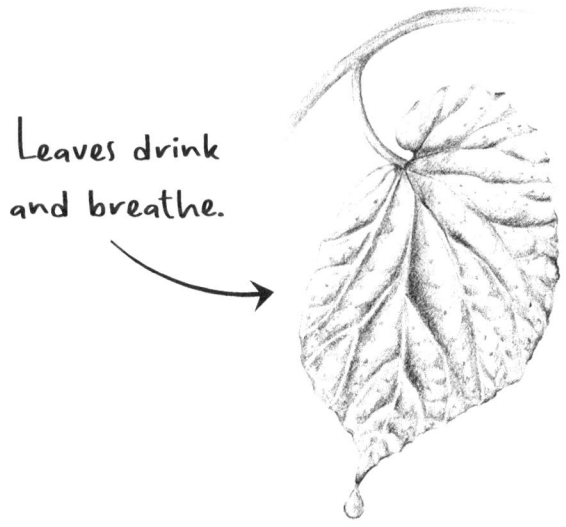

Leaves drink and breathe.

Wildlife Wong And The Fig Wasp

Have you heard that most of an iceberg is below the surface of the water? Well, in the same way, half a tree is underground. Trees send roots deep in the soil and spread them out, so they don't fall over.

A tree uses its roots to suck water and nutrients out of the ground into its trunk. Then it sends them all the way to its leaves (against gravity, which is pretty magical). Some of the water evaporates into the air. This is called **transpiration**. A big tree can drink a whole bathtub of water each day and when the water evaporates from its leaves, it makes the air very **humid**, or wet. The treetops trap the moist air and when it can't hold any more water, it causes mist or even rain. Have you ever noticed when you are walking in a forest, it feels cold and damp?

Trees breathe through their leaves too. Yes, they breathe, even though they don't have lungs! Using a little sun and water for energy, they breathe *in* carbon dioxide gas, which is part of the air, and they use it to grow. Then, they breathe *out* oxygen, another part of air, which they don't need. Humans (and most other animals) are

Wildlife Wong And The Fig Wasp

the opposite. We breathe *in* oxygen to help us stay alive, and we breathe *out* carbon dioxide. So, if you are sitting under a tree reading this book, you and the tree are helping each other stay alive. This is called a **symbiotic** relationship because you both win! If there are more people than trees (like in a capital city) the air is dirty because the trees can't keep up. That's a good reason to plant more trees, isn't it?

Is it time you put down your book for a minute and hugged a tree to say thank you?

Thank you trees!

PHOTOGRAPH: © WONG SIEW TE

Trees sometimes use their leaves to send messages to each other too. When some trees are being attacked by a swarm of nasty insects, they add different chemicals to the water going to the leaves. This changes their smell and warns other nearby trees that nasty insects are on their way. When the second tree smells the change (also through its leaves, because trees don't have noses), it adds chemicals to its own leaves that **repel** insects. I bet you won't look at a leaf the same way again!

What's special about fungi?

There are about 144,000 different types of fungi (which sounds like *fun guy*) and some delicious ones, like mushrooms, end up on your dinner plate. Another species of fungi called yeast makes your bread light and fluffy, and you might have seen fungi called mould, growing on something stuck at the back of your fridge just before you threw it out!

Wildlife Wong And The Fig Wasp

Do you remember the glowing fungi in the story? Some fungi create a chemical reaction in their bodies called **bioluminescence** (which sounds like *bio-lumi-nes-ence*). It makes them glow in the dark. Scientists think the light lures tiny insects which then help spread fungi spores (or seeds) the same way fig wasps spread pollen.

Other fungi spores fly around in the air unseen. They attach themselves to tiny salt crystals in the air, which attract water and rise to the top of the trees. The rainforest roof, or **canopy**, stops them rising further so they fall down, creating mist and rain. Isn't that amazing? Can you remember what type of relationship this is?

Fungi are important underground too. Tree roots are covered with tiny strands of fungi which help the tree absorb nutrients and, as a thank you, the tree shares its food with fungi.

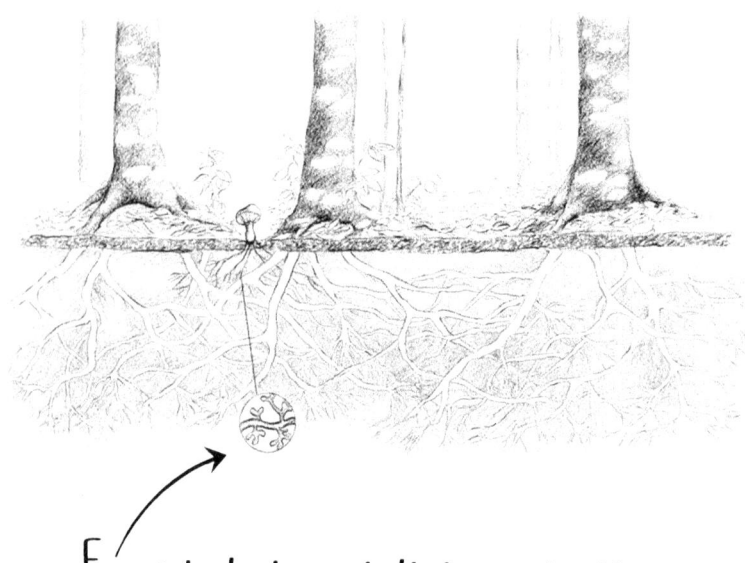

Fungi help trees talk to each other.

Just like the world wide web connects one computer to another until all the computers in the world are joined, the network of roots joins trees together. We use the world wide web to communicate with other people and trees use the 'wood wide web' of roots and fungi to communicate with each other. Sometimes mother trees even send food and water to their babies through the wood wide web. You can't do *that* through your screen!

How old are trees?

Have you ever heard someone say, 'I'd give anything to be young again?' Humans have been searching for a way to live longer and look younger for a very long time, but some trees have already solved the secret. They send fresh shoots up from their roots to the surface to grow a brand-new tree, which is really a part of the old tree. Then the old tree dies, and the new one goes on living a new life. This is called **cloning** or making a copy of yourself. The oldest cloned tree we have found so far is nicknamed *Pando*. It is in Utah, which is a state in America. It looks like an entire forest of 48,000 individual trees, but they have all grown from the same roots.

The roots are up to 14,000 years old!

So, don't be fooled… when you see a beautiful green **sapling**, or young tree, it might actually be older than your grandma!

Do some trees kill other trees?

One of the most amazing trees in the world is the fig tree. There are about 900 different fig trees, and some have a strange way of growing. A bird or animal drops, or poos, a seed on a branch in the canopy. Then the seed grows roots which weave down the trunk of the **host** tree, all the way to the soil. When they get there, the roots suck up nutrients and grow thicker and thicker around the base of the tree. The top of the fig tree grows thick and shades the host tree. There is not enough food or sunlight to feed both trees, and the host tree dies and rots away, leaving a hollow middle. Can you weave your fingers together? That's what **lattice** looks like, and the fig roots end up looking just like that.

Killer trees? Sounds like a horror movie, doesn't it? Perhaps that's why some fig trees are called strangler figs. The good news is, one fig tree can be home to up to 4,000 different plants and animals, and strangler fig trees are perfect trees for climbing, because they have heaps of footholds!

Wildlife Wong And The Fig Wasp

Photograph: © Wong Siew Te

Check out those roots!

What's cool about fig flowers?

The weirdest thing about fig trees is their flowers. If you picture a flower, I bet it has pretty, colourful petals, a sweet smell, a stem and perhaps a leaf? Those bright colours and smells attract insects who feed off the flower's sweet, sticky liquid called **nectar.** While the insects lick their favourite food, fine yellow pollen sticks to their body and they spread it to other flowers, or parts of the same flower. This **pollinates** the flower so it can grow seeds. Seeds are like tree babies. When animals eat the delicious fruit, and poo out the seeds, new trees can grow away from their parents.

Now imagine a flower bud that never opens. Most flower species would die if this happened because the insects wouldn't be able to get to the pollen and help them **procreate.** (Do you remember what that means?) But fig flowers just keep on growing bigger, hidden from view. All this growing would go to waste if they couldn't spread their pollen, and that's where the hero of our story comes in.

Fig wasps are superheros

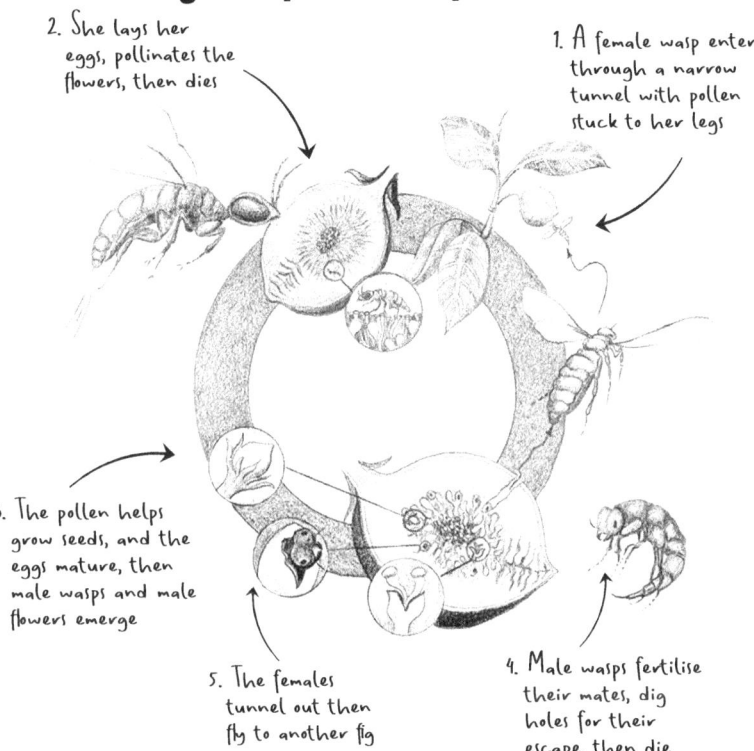

1. A female wasp enters through a narrow tunnel with pollen stuck to her legs
2. She lays her eggs, pollinates the flowers, then dies
3. The pollen helps grow seeds, and the eggs mature, then male wasps and male flowers emerge
4. Male wasps fertilise their mates, dig holes for their escape, then die
5. The females tunnel out then fly to another fig

Just like trees and fungi are best buddies, figs can't live without fig wasps, and fig wasps wouldn't survive without figs. Let me tell you more about how this works:

Fig wasps only grow 5mm long and they only live a couple of days. A female fig wasp lands on a fig flower. She is frantic because she only

Wildlife Wong And The Fig Wasp

has a few hours left to live, and heaps to do. She crawls around the **sphere** (or ball shape) until she finds a tiny tunnel entrance at the bottom of the fig. She squeezes her body into the hole. It is so tight, her wings get stuck, but there is no way to turn around, so she keeps going and leaves her wings behind. She won't need them anymore.

Eventually, the tunnel opens out into a dark, bumpy cavern. She's exhausted, but she can't stop yet. She drops an egg into each of the welcoming female flowers and leaves pollen from the male flowers from the place where she was born. Then she dies, knowing she has completed her mission.

Not long after, the male fig wasps hatch and mature. They know they will never get to see life outside the fig, so they don't bother growing wings. They only have two jobs. First, they search for the unhatched females and **impregnate** them before they even hatch. Then, in their dying act, they dig an escape route for their mates. By this time, the male flowers have created pollen and when the pregnant females hatch, it sticks to their legs. Without looking back, the females tunnel out, leaving the only world they have ever known behind.

Are there dead wasps in my figs?

The pollen left behind by the mother enables the female fig flowers to produce seeds, which takes up to two months. In that time, the dead fig wasps are **digested** (or eaten) by the fig using a powerful **enzyme**, which is a type of protein that speeds up the process. You aren't eating wasp bodies when you eat a fig, but the wasp bodies have helped make the fig taste delicious!

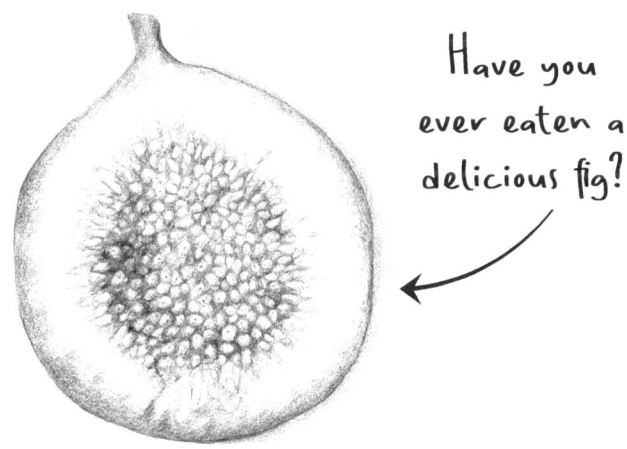

Have you ever eaten a delicious fig?

Why are fig trees better than supermarkets?

The newly emerged female fig wasps only have a few hours to find another suitable fig and tunnel inside to lay their own eggs. Because there isn't much time, fig trees grow their inside-out flowers all year round. And because there are fig fruits all year round, they feed more animals than any other type of tree in the world. Isn't that cool? Without fig trees, there would be no sun bears, or orangutans, or bearded pigs. They also provide homes for thousands of **invertebrates** (like beetles), **rodents** (like mice), **reptiles** (like snakes), **amphibians** (like frogs) and birds (like hornbills).

What happens if fig wasps become extinct?

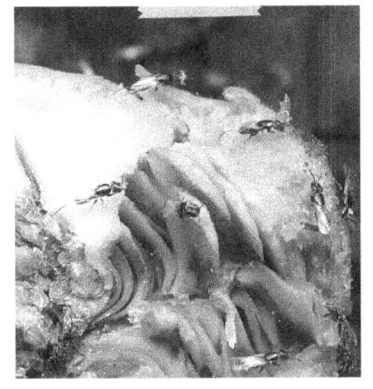

Save the fig wasp!

PHOTOGRAPH: © CHUN XING WONG

There are many different types of fig wasps, and many different types of fig trees. Some trees only have a relationship with one type of fig wasp, so if that type of fig wasp becomes extinct, the tree won't survive either. Global warming is threatening fig wasps because fig wasps don't live as long when it's hot outside. This means when the temperature rises, they have less time to find the right fig to lay their eggs.

Wildlife Wong And The Fig Wasp

In 1997 and 1998, a scientist called Rhett Harrison found that fig wasps were **locally extinct** in parts of Borneo because smoke had killed them. Some fires were natural forest fires and others were lit on purpose by people. Luckily, the wasps came back, but they are still in trouble because people still light fires to clear their land for planting.

Save fig trees!

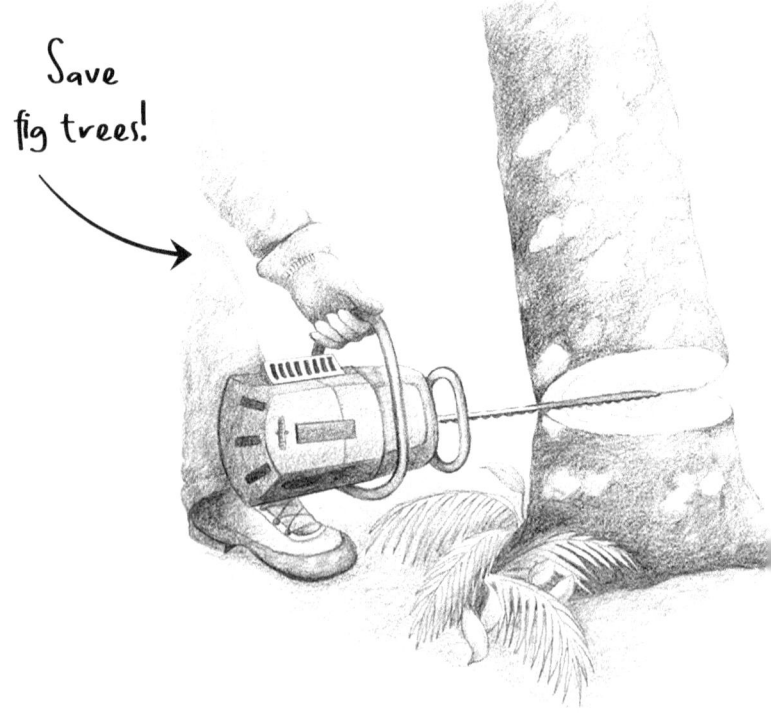

Flying frogs

Most frogs hang out in the water, but the bright green, teacup-sized Wallace's Flying Frog (which Wong heard booming) wasn't content with swimming. It decided the birds had the right idea, and the trees were the way to go. This frog spends almost all of its life in the trees, only coming down to mate and lay eggs. But that's not the only thing that makes it **unique**.

Most frogs use the webbing between their toes to help them swim fast, but the Wallace's Flying Frog uses its webbing to glide.

Frogs with superpowers!

Can you imagine being a slinky pit viper snake sneaking up on a frog along a high branch and thinking dinner is sorted? Then, suddenly, dinner jumps and spreads its legs out like a parachute, showing its yellow go-fast stripes. You'd be bummed, wouldn't you? I can almost hear the frog sighing with relief as it glides 15 metres to the next tree, lands softly on a leaf with its oversized toe pads, like Spiderman, folds away its black webbing, and walks away.

Vampires of the forest

Do you remember the part when Wildlife Wong was nearly attacked by a leech? Leeches are cunning blood-sucking squashy creatures which look like skinny slugs. They wander around the forest floor waiting for animals and humans to walk by, then they stand up on their tail and grab hold. They have three jaws and a hundred tiny teeth! When leeches bite, they inject **anaesthetic** into their prey, which stops the bite from hurting and allows them to suck up to 10 millilitres of blood before they are found out. Leech saliva also contains an **anticoagulant** (which sounds like *anti-co-ag-you-lant*). It is a type of chemical that stops the blood from clotting, or making a scab. That's how they can drink as much as they want. They really *are* vampires!

If you find a leech attached to your body, you can do what Wong did in the story. Or you can spray them with insect repellent or sprinkle them with salt. I always carry little takeaway packages of salt in my backpack when I walk in the rainforest.

Tricky illusionists

Is it a moth or a snake?

PHOTOGRAPH: © STEPHAN SICURELLA

Stick insects and chameleon lizards are really great at using camouflage to hide, but Atlas moths use a different illusion to escape being eaten. The Atlas moth is as big as Wong's hand

and the end of its paper-thin wings look like the heads of snakes. How does that help? Well, birds love tasty Atlas moths, and snakes love tasty birds. When a bird sees the moth, it can't tell if it should eat it or fly away. While it tries to figure out what to do, the moth escapes, leaving the bird without dinner. It's just another rainforest illusion.

What's the difference between a centipede and a millipede?

Scientists estimate there are 8,000 species of centipedes and 80,000 species of millipedes. Even if you only had one of each kind, that's a lot of legs! Do you know the difference between a centipede and a millipede? Sometimes there's a hint in the name of an animal. *Centi* is the Latin word for a hundred, *milli* means a thousand, and *ped* means foot. Does that mean centipedes have 100 legs, and millipedes have 1000 legs? Because of their name, many people think so but, some centipedes have more than 350 legs!

Wildlife Wong And The Fig Wasp

Both centipedes and millipedes are made of linking segments which look like medieval armour (like a knight wears). A centipede has two legs on each segment (one on each side). A millipede has four legs per segment (two on each side). Another difference is that centipedes usually eat insects, and millipedes feast on decomposing plants. Millipedes, like the pill millipede in the story, usually coil up in a ball when they are scared, but centipedes bite. It's a good idea to avoid centipedes!

Check out all those legs!

PHOTOGRAPH: © WONG SIEW TE

Wildlife Wong And The Fig Wasp

The animals and plants that live in the rainforest are pretty incredible, aren't they?

Over a very long time, they have worked out ingenious ways to live together. Our tiny hero, the fig wasp, and its friend the fig tree, have evolved together for 90 million years! Now that's a very long friendship.

Experiment 1: Make a Terrarium

(See videos at sarahrpye.com)

A terrarium is like a miniature rainforest. The plants drink water in the soil. They send it to their leaves where some of the water evaporates into the air. Do you remember what this process is called? The humid air is trapped inside the terrarium in the same way the tree canopy traps moisture in a rainforest. Water collects on the side of the jar, called **condensation**, and it dripples back down to the soil. Then the plants can drink it again. The water keeps circulating, which means it goes around in a circle, just like it does in a rainforest. But how do plants breathe if they are locked in a jar? Well, in the daytime, the plants breathe *in* carbon dioxide and breathe *out* oxygen. They do the opposite in the night, so the air circulates too. Isn't that incredible?

Are you ready to make your own terrarium?

You will need:

A large jar with a lid
Small stones or gravel
An old piece of fly screen
Horticultural charcoal
Potting mix
Small plants (you can get these from a nursery or dig them from your garden)
One or two decorative sticks or rocks

Chalk
Scissors
A spoon
Tongs
Paper towel

Steps:

1. Use the bottom of your jar to draw a circle on your fly screen with chalk
2. Cut out the circle and put it aside
3. Cover the bottom of your jar with a thin layer of small stones or gravel
4. Place the circle of fly screen on top of the stones. This makes sure the soil layer stays separate
5. Put a thin layer of charcoal on top of the fly screen. The charcoal will help filter the water
6. Next put potting mix on top of the charcoal until the jar is half full
7. Now get creative by planting your plants and placing sticks and decorative stones

8. Use a piece of paper towel to carefully wipe the inside of the glass
9. Now add 1-2 tablespoon of water to the jar and put the lid on tight

Hint:

Keep your terrarium indoors with some sunlight, but don't let it get too hot. If the jar is always foggy with condensation, it may have a little too much water. Simply take the lid off and wipe the inside of the glass with a paper towel then put the lid back on. Other than that, you shouldn't need to take the lid off!

Experiment 2: Make a Quadrat

What would you do if I took you to a field of wildflowers and asked you to count all the bees, or count all the yellow flowers? Could you do it? What if the bees moved? Or what if you lost track of your counting in the middle and had to start again?

Biologists would use a frame called a quadrat to count how many insects or flowers there are in a small square. Then they would multiply the answers by the number of quadrats they would need to cover the entire area to **estimate** the total.

There are many things you can do with a quadrat, like find out if more species of grass grow in a shady quadrat area or a sunny quadrat area, record the numbers of snails in your quadrat at the same time each day to see if the numbers are increasing or decreasing, or find out which is the most common type of shell on the beach. What do *you* want to discover?

Let's start by making a quadrat…

You will need:

An old picture frame (I got mine from a charity shop!)
10 thumbtacks
A hammer, plyers, and screwdriver
String
A tape measure (which is like a flexible ruler)
A pencil, notebook and ruler

Steps:

1. Take the photo and glass out of the frame using pliers and a screwdriver if needed. (You may need an adult to help you with this bit.)
2. Measure the long side of the opening using the measuring tape. Fold the measuring tape in half to find half the length and mark it on the long side of the opening.
3. Fold the measuring tape again (into four) to find a quarter the length of the long side and mark it on the long side of the opening from each end. You now have marks at a quarter, a half and three quarters the length.
4. Do the same on the other long side.
5. Measure the short side of the opening using the measuring tape. This time, fold the measuring tape in three and mark one third and two thirds of the length on the short side of the opening.
6. Do the same on the other short side.
7. Hammer thumbtacks into each mark.

Wildlife Wong And The Fig Wasp

8. Tie the end of the ball of string to the thumbtack closest to a corner on the long side.
9. Stretch the string across the opening to the thumbtack closest to the corner on the other long side.
10. Next, stretch the string along the frame on the same side to the next thumbtack and wrap it round.
11. Now stretch the string across the opening to the opposite thumbtack and wrap again.
12. Repeat numbers 10 and 11 until you end up in the far corner from where you started and tie off your string. Cut it.
13. Tie another piece of string to the thumbtack closest to the corner on the SHORT side. Repeat numbers 9, 10, and 11 until you get to the last thumbtack, then tie off your string.
14. Do you have a grid with 12 smaller rectangles?

Now you can use your quadrat for science!

1. Choose a place on the grass, dirt or beach you want to observe.
2. Put the quadrat down flat.
3. Choose what you want to count. It may be plants or animals.
4. Draw a map of your quadrat on a piece of paper using a pencil and ruler.
5. Number the 12 rectangles.
6. Write, or draw, the number of specimens in each rectangle.

New words

Some of the words or phrases in this book are bold. Here's what they mean. They are in alphabetical order. If a word (or phrase) starts with A, AN or THE, it is a noun (a person, place or thing). If it starts with TO BE, it is a verb (a doing word). An adverb describes (or adds to) a verb, and an adjective describes (or adds to) a noun. Once you learn a new word, try using it!

An amphibian — a class of cold-blooded animal that includes frogs and toads

An anaesthetic — a substance that stops you feeling pain

An antenna — a wire device that transmits or receives radio signals

An anticoagulant — a substance that stops blood from clotting or getting thick

Wildlife Wong And The Fig Wasp

Biodiversity (noun) — the variety of plants and animals in a habitat

Bioluminescence (noun) — when an animal or plant uses a chemical reaction to glow in the dark

Biomimicry (noun) — when humans copy the natural world to design other things

A **buttress root** — a very thick root above the ground that holds a tree up

Camouflage (noun) — colours that blend with the surroundings

The **canopy** — the top of the tree or trees

To **clone** — to make an exact copy of something

Condensation (noun) — water which collects on a cold surface from humid air

To **coordinate** — to work together

A **corpse** — a dead animal or human body

Debris (noun) — scattered rubbish

To **digest** — to eat something and break it down using chemicals

An **ecologist** — a scientist who studies how plants, animals and humans live together

Wildlife Wong And The Fig Wasp

An enzyme — a natural substance that creates a chemical reaction

To estimate — to guess using your knowledge

Excrement (noun) — poo

Faeces (noun) — another word for poo!

A famine — a time when there is not enough food

Fauna (noun) — another name for animals

Flora (noun) — another name for plants

Foliage (noun) — leaves

The girth — the distance around the waist

To glimpse — to look

A host — the animal or plant a parasite lives on

Humid (adjective) — describes air that holds a lot of water vapour

To impregnate — to fertilise something, or make it pregnant

Indicated (verb) — showed

An invertebrate — an animal without a backbone

A laboratory — a place where scientists work

Larvae — immature insects before they become adults, like caterpillars or maggots

A lattice — an interlaced or weaved structure

To be locally extinct — to have disappeared in a local habitat

Longitudinal (adjective) — a study done over a long period of time

Malnourished (adjective) — really thin and unwell

A mammal — a warm-blooded animal with hair whose babies are born alive, not in an egg

Mass fruiting (noun) — when all the trees produce flowers and fruit at the same time

Nectar (noun) — a sticky, sugary liquid in plants or fruit

To be nocturnal — to be awake at night and sleep in the daytime

An observation — looking at things in detail

To pollinate — moving pollen from one flow to another

Predation (noun) — when one animal eats another

Preservation (noun) — keeping things the same or keeping yourself alive

A procession — a line of people or animals moving in the same direction

Procreation (noun) — the process of having babies

Putrid (adjective) — describing something that smells bad

To repel — to make something go away

A reptile — a scaly cold-blooded animal (includes snakes, lizards and turtles)

A rodent — an animal that gnaws with teeth that don't stop growing (includes rats and mice)

A sapling — a young tree

A scat — an animal poo

To scuttle — to run away fast

A sphere — a ball shape

Symbiotic — a type of relationship which is good for everyone

Topographic (adjective) — a topographic map shows natural things like hills and stream, not roads and buildings

Transpiration (noun) — the way plants breathe out water vapour

To be unique — one of a kind!

Unison (adjective) — doing something together

To witness — to watch, see something

Do you want to read more?

Wildlife Wong is lucky. He has adventures will all kinds of animals!
Why not check out these stories next?

Don't forget, you can find videos of the experiments on my website:

⊕ **www.sarahrpye.com**

Make your own book

Would you like to make your own book? If you go to my website, www.sarahrpye.com, you can download free pages to make your own Nature Journal and a template for making a cool cover. Does that sounds like fun? Don't forget to send me a photo when you are done!

Wildlife Wong And The Fig Wasp

You will need:

- A printer
- Brown paper
- A ruler
- A pencil
- Scissors
- String
- A large needle
- An ice pick (and someone to help you)

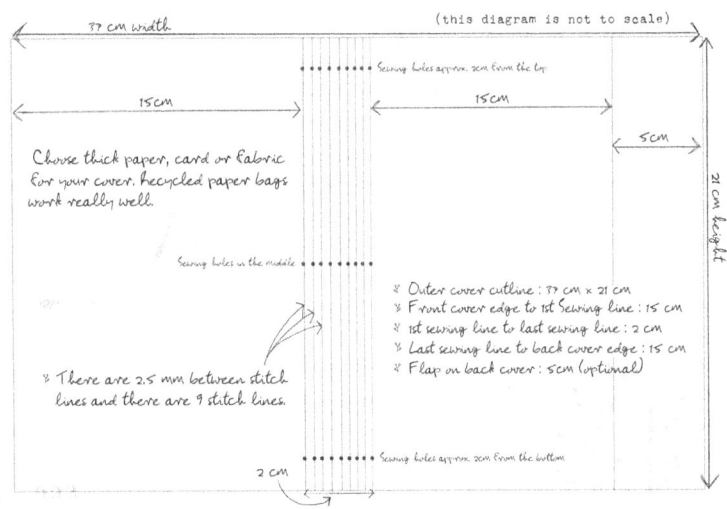

Here is the cover template which you can download online

Wildlife Wong And The Fig Wasp

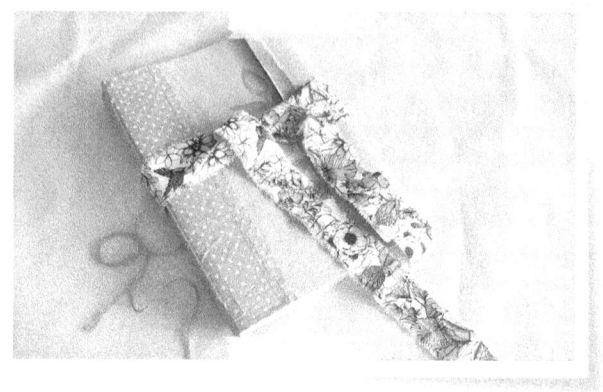

You can decorate your
cover any way you like!

Do you want to help protect tiny animals?

Here are a few ideas:

- Lend this book to your friends so they can learn about fig wasps and other animals too
- Do a school project on the rainforest and use the facts in this book
- Download your free **Nature Journal** at www.sarahrpye.com
- If you waste less and buy less, less rainforest needs to be cut down
- Volunteer with a conservation group in your own area – the entire environment needs help, not just in Borneo!
- If you are old enough, connect with me on Instagram or Facebook
- Send me an email at www.sarahrpye.com to share more ideas!

For teachers and parents:

Sarah Pye loves visiting schools both in person and online to teach kids more about the rainforest. For more information visit:

🌐 **www.sarahrpye.com**

This book is printed on demand (POD) which reduces waste and saves our trees.

www.ingramcontent.com/pod-product-compliance
Lightning Source LLC
Chambersburg PA
CBHW071839290426
44109CB00017B/1873